HEARTWORK

Also by Maggie Victor

The Choice for Love
Meeting the Challenges of a Heartfelt Life

A timely, compassionate, and unique vision of the human challenges to be met in the passage from fear, through the heart chakra, into Love.

You can visit Maggie at Antenesca's website at www.antenesca.com to read more of her writings and to subscribe to our Heartletter.

HEARTWORK

Accepting an Imperfect Life as the Perfect Path to Love

MAGGIE VICTOR

ANTENESCA

Antenesca Publishing
Montreal

Legal Deposit – Bibliothèque nationale du Québec, 2003
              – National Library of Canada, 2003

CANADIAN CATALOGUING IN PUBLICATION DATA

Victor, Maggie, 1947–

Heartwork: accepting an imperfect life as the perfect path to love: your personal journey of healing through the heart

ISBN 0-9689200-1-2

1. Spiritual life. 2. Spiritual healing.
3. Love – Religious aspects. 4. Spiritual life – Problems, exercises, etc.
5. Spiritual healing – Problems, exercises, etc. 6. Self-help techniques.
I. Victor, Maggie, 1947- . Choice for love. II. Title.

BL626.4.V52 2002 SUPPL.   291.5'677   C2002-941770-8

Cover design by David Drummond
Cover and interior illustration by David Drummond and Gail McGowan
Editing by Jill R. Hughes
Typesetting by Yolande Martel

Printed and bound in Canada on acid-free paper

To contact us:
Antenesca Publishing
31 Pacific Avenue
Senneville, Québec, Canada, H9X 1A6
www.antenesca.com

Contents

Preface

As I was writing *The Choice for Love*, the idea for this workbook was a persistent presence that accompanied me through that first manuscript and would stand aside only temporarily once I promised to bring it into form as soon as possible. The desire of Love to create a book extended immediately to the desire to engage others in their own creativity.

Knowing what we know is one thing. Living what we know is quite another. The gap between knowing and living is the healing work we choose for ourselves in this lifetime. Spirit, while transcendent and mystical, is also practical in Its desire to be manifest. It is *we* who can consciously manifest Spirit through our choices, our intentions, our words, our actions, and it is in relationship that we enter the healing arena of the heart. Our life is our healing.

Perceiving the situations, relationships, and challenges of my life as the gifted means to a joyous end enabled me to see everything differently. Instead of avoiding and resisting people and circumstances that evoked fear in my life, I began to experiment with the tools that are offered in this workbook. I also used this form of consciousness-raising with students and clients over many years. The benefits and healing potential of these exercises were unmistakably practical and humanized the concepts of the spiritual path.

For those who have made the choice for Love, *Heartwork* is offered as a tool to assist you in the grounded reality of the path of the heart. It is a way of beginning the journey through your heart to Self-knowledge and to discovering your unique expression of compassion and service. We take this journey together as we explore and heal our hearts and cocreate a place of safety for the Heart on this planet.

Maggie Victor
April 11, 2002

Acknowledgments

The joy of cocreation is to experience our union with one another through the joint manifestation of vision and talent. The fruits of relationship, the gifts we give together to the world extend beyond the limits of our immediate perception and connect us through the heart with others of like mind and soul.

The cocreators of this workbook are:

Michèle Cyr, publisher, whose talent for creating the perfect form of a manuscript was dedicated in countless hours to the layout design and final presentation of *Heartwork*.

David Drummond, who once again brought inspiration and vision to the artistic design of the cover.

Jill R. Hughes, editor, who enthusiastically worked to preserve the flow of structure and consistency in this workbook.

The clients, students, and workshop participants, who over the course of the last twelve years have joined with me in the exercises and visualizations of *Heartwork*. The generous and courageous sharing of their own path of the heart has been the true creative inspiration for this workbook.

Introduction

Welcome to *Heartwork,* your personal journey through the inner sanctuary of your own heart. This workbook has been designed to accompany you step-by-step through the chambers of your heart and to offer you tools for some of the challenges that you will meet on the path from fear to Love. Here, in the time that you devote to the deepening of your Self-knowledge and to the contemplation of your life's meaning, you will give yourself the opportunity to heal the blocks to Love. You will begin to awaken to the possibilities of joy and the fulfillment of your potential for Love, happiness, and purpose.

Your own heart is the only heart you can heal. Your own heart is the sanctuary where the Source of Love, the Source of Wisdom, and the Source of Truth enter to unite with your human experience in a compassionate understanding that *your life is your healing.* Your heart is the meeting place of the human and the Divine. It is this level of integration of the personal self and the spiritual Self that enables you to make the choice for Love manifest and real. This integration, this wholeness of heart brings extraordinary passion into ordinary life and illuminates the meaning and application of the spiritual path on planet Earth.

As you experience the thoughts, exercises, and meditations of this workbook, you will come to realize that the time you take to enter the sanctuary of your heart becomes sacred. As you enter this level of growth and commit to transforming a fear-based life into an expression of Love, you are taking the responsibility that you alone can fulfill. Taking that responsibility is true empowerment, as it offers again and again the choice between fear and Love. Each choice for Love in the temptation of fear strengthens you, heals your heart, and increases the power of compassion in your life.

The journey of consciousness begins with looking honestly at your life exactly as it is and practicing presence with it. In this, your personal *Heartwork* journal, you will have the opportunity to deepen your contemplation of all that is in your life right now and to use everything that is present as a means to discovering the power of your heart. In solitude and silence you will begin the process of Self-discovery. After you have explored these exercises individually, you may seek the benefits of sharing this work with others in a group setting. Meeting to exchange experiences and insights with those who are engaged in their own heartwork can enrich your path and enlarge your understanding of the choice for Love. To meet in a group setting, it is suggested that members take turns leading or facilitating the group and that the commitment to confidentiality and honesty is affirmed.

Preparation for Heartwork

Centering

Giving yourself the gifts of silence and solitude to work with the exercises is the way you honor your path of the heart. As you begin to engage in your personal heartwork, you will discover the times and situations that best support your contemplation. There will be a time of day when you experience increased energy and greater clarity, perhaps early in the morning. There will be situations and physical environments that seem to enable a peaceful quiet time. Finding the time and place to center yourself for writing, drawing, and thinking can take some experimentation. Finding the time and place to heal your heart in the midst of a busy life requires commitment. Allow yourself to discover your own unique way to take the time and space you need, and allow these dimensions to change and increase as you desire. This work is about Self-knowledge, and knowing what works easily and naturally in your healing process is part of that understanding.

As you sit with the workbook and prepare to do an exercise, take a few minutes to relax, close your eyes, and breathe slowly and deeply. Allow the breath to go right down into your solar plexus and belly. Imagine that as you breathe in, you are taking in peace and safety and clarity, and that as you breathe out, you are releasing tension and anxiety. Follow your own breath for a few minutes until you feel ready to begin.

After you have finished the work that you want to do at that time, take the time to again follow your breath. As the breath descends into the solar plexus and belly, imagine that you are breathing in harmony, healing, and light. As you breathe out, imagine that you are exuding acceptance and gratitude.

At all points in the process of healing the heart, you will consciously experience your thoughts and feelings. Just allow them to surface and write them out without judgment or editing. This is the meaning of honesty. As you allow the experience of *all* of your feelings, you are practicing courage. If at times the feelings seem overwhelming, you can return to the breath while you stay with the feeling. This is the practice of presence.

As you move deeply into the internal work of healing your heart, you will be engaging your imagination, your will, and your feelings. Although much of the work may be conducted in solitude, you are joining many others who are participating in their own heartwork because they too have answered the call to Love. At the same time, you are being joined by Spirit to support and uphold your journey out of fear. As you become more and more conscious of the opportunities to practice your heartwork in your life, you may find that not only do you look at everything differently, but also that unexpected synchronicities provide assistance and guidance. Your external reality will mirror back to you the changes that are taking place internally. You can trust that Life provides everything you need to heal your heart and that the relationships, events, and circumstances you are working with are perfect.

The workbook will follow the stages of healing outlined in *The Choice for Love: Meeting the Challenges of a Heartfelt Life.* These stages are (1) Awakening, (2) Healing of the Heart, and (3) Heart in Relationship. At each stage you will have to the opportunity to make use of visualization, journaling, and the drawing of symbols and images, should you choose to do so. You will be exploring and recording your levels of experience at the physical, emotional, mental, and soul levels. Allow yourself to use various colored crayons, pens, or pastels and to use some of the blank pages in your journal to create your own images of healing and joy.

Visualization

The technique of visualization is a very useful tool in the healing process. In a state of deep relaxation we use our imagination, feelings, and will to guide our own energy and to gain Self-knowledge. Many of the exercises in this book will make use of visualization, because your creative imagination—along with your feelings and the direction of your will—is what creates your life. Take as long as you like with each step in the process, and accept what you experience without judgment. Have a sense of allowing rather than forcing, and record without editing the thoughts, feelings, and images that come from your own psyche.

The following steps outlined here are recommended for each visualization that you do throughout the workbook. You may read through all of the steps before beginning, and then allow your experience to evolve without being concerned about the structure of the exercise. If you prefer, you could have someone read the steps to you, or you could record them and play them back to guide you during a visualization.

1. Arrange a time of quiet, when you know that you will be uninterrupted, in an environment where you feel safe and comfortable.

2. Sit comfortably in a chair with both feet on the ground, or in meditation position (lotus), or lie down comfortably on the floor. Whichever position

you choose, become aware of your spine. Try to keep the spine straight, but not rigid. As you arrange your spine in a straight line, your body will naturally align itself. If you are not sure of your position, just imagine your spine, at its core, as a thin golden wire. Like any wire, its natural position is straight but flexible and relaxed.

3. Allow your eyes to close and allow your face to relax.

4. Allow your breath to deepen. You are opening your solar plexus and your lower belly. You are drawing the breath deeper and deeper into your body and allowing that breath to expand your belly outward. As you exhale, empty completely and pause briefly in that emptiness before drawing in the next breath.

5. Imagine that you are breathing in safety and peace deeper and deeper into your body, and that on the out-breath you are letting go of tension and anxiety.

6. Allow the safety and peace to relax your muscles and bones, and observe any places in the body that seem to be tense or where the breath has difficulty moving through. Just ease around the areas and allow the breath to flow.

7. When you feel a sense of safety and peace and the flow of breath is well established, allow your attention to gently move to the pictures that are floating through your mind. Just allow them to float like images on a movie screen until the screen becomes clear.

Now you are ready to use your imagination to focus on the exercise you are working on.

PART I

AWAKENING

When we begin to bring the power of consciousness to the experiences of the present moment, we bring Love to that moment.

The Choice for Love
The Heart as Meeting Place

I

The Heart as Meeting Place

. . . The seat of integration is not the intellect, but the heart.

The Choice for Love
The Heart as Meeting Place

The acceptance and integration of our human path and our Divine under-standing takes place at the heart level of our Spiritual Path. Here we bring together apparent opposites, our Higher Selves and our lower selves, the best in us and the worst, our greatest joy and our most acute pain. This union of the human and the Divine in our own hearts brings meaning to *all* of our journey and empowers us to follow the path of the Heart.

VISUALIZATION I

1. After completing the seven-step preparation for visualization (pp. 17–18), with eyes still closed, allow yourself to imagine that you can see your entire body from head to toe as you feel your breath moving freely through every part of your body.

2. Allow yourself to become aware of your heart place—the area that includes shoulders, mid-chest, both front and back. See this area as the midpoint of your body. Imagine it as a crossroads between your connection to the Divine and your human experience.

3. Imagine that your human experience is a vital red-colored energy that is moving from the ground through your feet and traveling up through your legs, your lower belly, and your solar plexus into your heart place. Feel the red color flooding the lower body with warmth and vitality. Feel its vigor entering the heart place as the color red infuses the area of the middle chest.

4. Now imagine that Divine Energy is showering white light, which is pouring down through the crown of your head. Feel this light as peace and joy filling the entire head and face, flowing down through the neck and shoulders, and flooding into your heart area. Feel your heart resting and easing into this white light.

5. Allow yourself to see the red and the white energies moving around in your heart until they gradually and gently combine into the color pink.

6. You are watching this beautiful pink energy endlessly filling the heart and starting to overflow into the rest of your body. You can see the pink traveling upward from the heart, through the shoulders, into the head and face, and out the crown of the head. You can also see the pink traveling downward through the solar plexus, the lower belly, the legs, through the feet, and into the ground.

7. Stay with this experience as long as you like. When you are ready, gently return your attention to the breath. As you listen to the sound of your breathing, become aware of any other sounds that may be in your environment. Allow your attention to focus on the physical sensations of your surroundings. Have a sense of returning to the room you are in. When you are ready, open your eyes.

Heartwork

My Experience with the Heart as Meeting Place

Physical sensations:

Emotions and feelings:

Thoughts and insights:

Images (pictures, visions, symbols):

My Experience with the Heart as Meeting Place

A drawing of a symbol or image that I saw during my visualization:

2

Acceptance

Your Life is your healing.

The Choice for Love
The Heart as Meeting Place

Acceptance does not mean that we necessarily like what is happening in our life right now. Acceptance means that we are willing to look clearly at the situations, relationships, and challenges of our life without avoiding or denying them. The following exercise will give you an opportunity to begin practicing presence with all that is in your life right now.

What I accept about my life:

What I do not accept about my life:

My Experience of Acceptance

Physical sensations:

Emotions and feelings:

Thoughts and insights:

Images (pictures, visions, symbols):

My Experience of Nonacceptance

Physical sensations:

Emotions and feelings:

Thoughts and insights:

Images (pictures, visions, symbols):

Integration of Acceptance and Nonacceptance

What I would like to keep in my life:

Integration of Acceptance and Nonacceptance

What I would like to let go of in my life:

3

From Morality into Integrity

*From the fragmentation and control ethic of morality
into the unshakeable truth of integrity is a passage
directly through the chambers of the heart.*

The Choice for Love
From Morality into Integrity

The following exercises are offered to enable you to distinguish between Love and fear, between your ego-personality and your soul, as you evaluate the inner influences on your daily perceptions and decisions. Becoming aware of the difference between morality and integrity enables us to consciously choose which we will call upon to create our life.

For the focus of this next set of explorations choose one situation in your life where you are experiencing conflict.

The way things should be: →

What happened in the past: →

← *The way things are:*

← *What is happening now:*

What I believe I must do:　→

What my rational self wants for me:　→

← *What I really want to do:*

← *What my heart desires:*

What I think I should feel:

What I really feel:

My Experience of Morality

Physical sensations:

Emotions and feelings:

Thoughts and insights:

Images (pictures, visions, symbols):

My Experience of Integrity

Physical sensations:

Emotions and feelings:

Thoughts and insights:

Images (pictures, visions, symbols):

Describe a life shaped by morality:

Describe a life shaped by integrity:

PART II

HEALING OF THE HEART

The courage to undertake the knowing of ourselves, all of ourselves, will take us into the places of the heart that need to be seen clearly and healed. In this deepening of self-knowledge, we are moving through the heart to discover our power to love.

The Choice for Love
Into the Sanctuary of the Heart

4

Into the Sanctuary of the Heart

As the secrets of the heart are revealed through this inward journey,
the blocks to Love are fully seen and transformed.
This transformation engages consciousness and imagination.

The Choice for Love
Into the Sanctuary of the Heart

This next section of *Heartwork* will take you into the deep exploration of the inner sanctuary of your heart. Here we will be using the technique of deep relaxation and visualization to explore and heal the separations and divisions we experience at this level of spiritual and human growth. In the journey through these divisions, we move through the back heart, in which lies our knowledge of the shadow; through the front heart, in which lies the knowledge of Love's potential; and through the gap in between the front and back heart, in which lie all our fears of union and love.

As you move through the chambers of the divided heart, you will meet the teachers of the heart, who each have messages and energy with which to assist you in your journey to wholeness. These teachers at first appear in the guise of not-love and will work with you to go beneath these appearances to the Love that is behind the fear. As you enter into dialogue with these teachers, you will be learning the necessary lessons that enable you to bring compassion to your own life and to others.

As you write about these encounters and all the feelings and thoughts they evoke, give yourself permission to accept without judgment whatever you see and feel. These experiences are universal and common to all of us. They cross the boundaries of time and space, culture and creed, age and gender, race and religion. In these experiences you are connecting to the common heart of humanity, and you are preparing the sanctuary of your heart to receive the Heart of the Divine.

As you move through the visualizations and then write about them in detail, allow yourself to revisit certain teachers if you feel the need to. If at any time the process seems too challenging, give yourself permission to stop and to return another time. Respect your own rhythm and resist the temptation to judge or evaluate your progress.

An Image of Your Heart

VISUALIZATION 2

Refer to the seven-step visualization process in Preparation for Heartwork (pp. 17–18) before entering into this next visualization.

1. In a state of deep relaxation, with your eyes closed, gently bring your attention to the area of your upper chest and breasts, shoulders, shoulder blades, and upper back.

2. Become aware of the physical sensations in these parts of your body. Have a sense of your heartbeat and your breath.

3. Staying connected to these sensations, allow yourself to see what the sanctuary of your heart looks like. It may take the form of a house, a church, a cathedral, a temple, a place in the forest, anything at all. Allow it to take whatever form it wishes.

4. Allow yourself to enter and explore this sanctuary—its colors, its textures, its construction, its chambers. Allow yourself to see it from all viewpoints—above, below, behind, and in front.

5. Now you are watching as the front and back of the sanctuary are being divided from top to bottom. As the front is separated from the back, the chambers of the sanctuary also divide into half-chambers.

6. There is a now a gap between the front and back of this heart place. Allow yourself to see and feel the gap between the front and the back.

7. Stay with this image and explore it for as long as you wish.

8. When you are ready to leave, bring your attention back to the breath. Become aware of the physical sensations throughout your body. Become aware of the sounds in your environment. When you are ready, open your eyes.

My Experience of Exploring the Sanctuary of My Heart

Physical sensations:

Emotions and feelings:

Thoughts and insights:

Images (pictures, visions, symbols):

My Experience of Exploring the Sanctuary of My Heart

Detailed description of the image(s) of my heart place:

5

Meeting the Teachers of the Back Heart

*It is the work of the heart that unites us all in
our common humanity, and it is in the healing of
the heart that we become one with one another.*

The Choice for Love
Teachers of the Heart I

As we meet with the teachers of the back heart, we are working with emotional experiences that we often judge and find hard to accept. Jealousy, anger, loneliness, and the misuse of power are forms of fear that disguise the love we all have deep within. As we meet these disguised teachers, as we courageously face what seems to be negativity, we are challenging these illusions and asking for the truth behind them to be revealed. Rather than repressing or denying these experiences, we are undertaking to learn from them so that we no longer need these defenses. We are redirecting the energy from fear to Love.

As we become conscious of the energy sources of these disguises in the back heart and allow for their transformation, we are illuminating the once darkened chambers of our heart. We are releasing creative energy from the prison of the self-image to the expression of our essence. The knowledge of the back heart, when explored and unified with the front heart, becomes the wisdom we need to bring mature compassion to our human path.

Jealousy

Allow yourself to remember a situation in which you experienced jealousy, or think of what evokes jealousy in your life right now. Whatever the apparent reasons that you believe are causing your jealousy, allow yourself to remain focused on the feeling experience. Your real exploration is not the outside cause, but rather the experience of jealousy itself. Take the time to observe how this experience moves through your body, what feelings are associated with it, what thoughts come to you, and what forms jealousy takes in your life.

Describe the experience of jealousy in as much detail as you can.

Physical sensations of jealousy:

Feelings and emotions associated with jealousy:

Thoughts and insights about jealousy:

Images and memories:

Meeting the Teacher of Jealousy

VISUALIZATION 3

Prepare for visualization by following the seven-step visualization process in Preparation for Heartwork (pp. 17–18).

In a state of deep relaxation allow your inner eye to envision a safe place where you can meet with jealousy. Allow this teacher to appear in whatever form occurs. You are observing this teacher carefully and taking note of all the details of its presence.

> What does your jealousy look like?
> Do you see any colors or symbols?
> If jealousy appeared as a person, what would that person look like?
> Male or female?   Age?   Clothing?
> Movement, action?

Allow yourself to fully experience this presence. When you have the feeling that you are familiar enough with this presence to recognize it any time again, ask your jealousy to speak to you, and in turn you can speak to your jealousy. Experience this dialogue for as long as you wish.

> What is your jealousy communicating to you? What is its message?

When you feel that the dialogue is finished for now, thank this presence for its message and release it. Allow your attention to return to your breathing. Follow the sound and movement of your breath, and become aware of the sounds in your environment. Have a sense of fully returning to the room you are in, and when you are ready, open your eyes.

My Experience with the Teacher of Jealousy

Write a detailed physical description of the appearance of jealousy:

Describe your feelings during this encounter:

Describe the behaviors or actions expressed by jealousy:

My Experience with the Teacher of Jealousy

Record in detail the dialogue that took place between you and jealousy:

Desire

Behind the disguise of jealousy stands the teacher of desire. The experience of jealousy is a sign that somehow the true desire of your heart has been sacrificed and denied. The return through jealousy to the core of desire begins the healing of separation from our true path. It is a willingness to learn our lessons through joy rather than through pain. It is the courage to find out what we really want to do with our lives, not what we think we *should* want. It is the key to the vision of our life's mission and the personal responsibility to know and fulfill our highest potential.

Describe the experience of desire in as much detail as you can.

Physical sensations of desire:

Feelings and emotions associated with desire:

Thoughts and insights about desire:

Images and memories:

Meeting the Teacher of Desire

Prepare for visualization by following the seven-step visualization process in Preparation for Heartwork (pp. 17–18).

In a state of deep relaxation, with eyes closed, allow your attention to focus again on the safe place where you met with jealousy. Invite the teacher of jealousy to reappear, and when this presence is fully with you, take a few minutes to observe any changes that have taken place in this aspect.

When you feel that communication between you has opened fully, request this teacher of jealousy to reveal itself to you as the teacher of desire. Observe the transformation, and remain present as the changes occur. Note any colors or symbols that accompany these changes.

You are taking note of every detail of the appearance of desire.

What does your desire look like?
Do you see any colors or symbols?
If desire came to you as a person, what would that person look like?
Male or female?
Age?
Clothing?
Movement, action?

When you feel completely familiar with this aspect and know that you would recognize it again any time, ask your desire to speak to you. If you choose, you may also speak to desire. Experience this dialogue for as long as you wish.

What does the teacher of desire wish to communicate to you? What message does it bring?

When you sense that the dialogue is finished for now, thank this presence for its message and release it. Allow your attention to return to your breathing. Follow the sound and movement of your breath, and become aware of the sounds in your environment. Have a sense of fully returning to the room you are in, and when you are ready, open your eyes.

My Experience with the Teacher of Desire

Write a detailed description of the appearance of desire:

Describe your feelings during this encounter:

Describe the behaviors or actions expressed by desire:

My Experience with the Teacher of Desire

Record in detail the dialogue that took place between you and desire:

Anger

Allow yourself to remember a situation in which you experienced anger, or think of what evokes anger in your life right now. As you remember the apparent causes of anger, allow your attention to turn to the actual feelings you are experiencing. You are focusing on the sensations of anger rather than on the external situation. Take the time to observe how this experience moves through your body. What other feelings surface with the experience of anger? What thoughts come to you, and what forms does anger take in your life?

Describe the experience of anger in as much detail as you can.

Physical sensations of anger:

Feelings and emotions associated with anger:

Thoughts and insights about anger:

Images and memories:

Meeting the Teacher of Anger

Prepare for visualization by following the seven-step visualization process in Preparation for Heartwork (pp. 17–18).

In a state of deep relaxation allow your inner eye to envision a safe place where you can meet with anger. Allow this teacher to appear in whatever form manifests. You are observing this teacher carefully and taking note of all the details of its presence.

What does your anger look like?
Do you see any colors or symbols?
If anger appeared as a person, what would that person look like?
Male or female?   Age?   Clothing?
Movement, action?

Allow yourself to fully experience this presence. When you have the feeling that you are familiar and comfortable with this presence, ask your anger to speak to you, and in turn you may speak to your anger. Experience this dialogue for as long as you wish.

What is your anger communicating to you? What is its message?

When you sense that the dialogue is finished for now, thank this presence for its message and release it. Allow your attention to return to your breathing. Follow the sound and movement of your breath. Become aware of the sounds in your physical environment. Have a sense of fully returning to the room you are in, and when you are ready, open your eyes.

My Experience with the Teacher of Anger

Write a detailed description of the appearance of anger:

Describe your feelings during this encounter:

Describe the behaviors or actions expressed by anger:

My Experience with the Teacher of Anger

Record in detail the dialogue that took place between you and anger:

Passion

Behind the disguise of anger stands the teacher of passion. It can take time to understand that anger has only one root cause, and that cause is our separation from our true passion, our Divine Nature. Denied or repressed passion does not disappear; its energy is merely redirected and expressed as anger. The willingness to return through anger to the core of passion is the willingness to reclaim the creative life force within and the courage to allow that vitality to change our path into a more authentic expression of our true Self.

Describe the experience of passion in as much detail as you can.

Physical sensations of passion:

Feelings and emotions associated with passion:

Thoughts and insights about passion:

Images and memories:

Meeting the Teacher of Passion

VISUALIZATION 6

Prepare for visualization by following the seven-step visualization process in Preparation for Heartwork (pp. 17–18).

In a state of deep relaxation, with eyes closed, allow your attention to focus again on the safe place where you met with anger. Invite the teacher of anger to reappear, and when this presence is fully with you, take a few minutes to observe any changes that have taken place in this aspect.

When you sense that communication between you is well established, request this teacher of anger to reveal itself to you as the teacher of passion. Observe the transformation and remain present as the changes evolve. Note any colors or symbols that accompany these changes.

You are taking note of every detail of the appearance of passion.

What does your passion look like?
If passion came to you as a person, what would that person look like?
Male or female?
Age?
Clothing?
Movement, action?

When you feel completely familiar with the teacher of passion and know that you would recognize this presence again any time, ask your passion to speak to you. If you choose, you may also speak to passion. Experience this dialogue for as long as you wish.

What is your passion communicating to you? What message does passion bring?

When you sense that the dialogue is complete for now, thank this teacher for its message of passion and release it. Allow your attention to return to your breathing. Follow the sound and movement of your breath, and become aware of the sounds in your environment. Have a sense of fully returning to the room you are in, and when you are ready, open your eyes.

My Experience with the Teacher of Passion

Write a detailed description of the appearance of passion:

Describe your feelings during this encounter:

Describe the behaviors or actions expressed by passion:

My Experience with the Teacher of Passion

Record in detail the dialogue that took place between you and passion:

Loneliness

Allow yourself to remember a time in your life when you felt alone and lonely. Think of the situations in your life right now that evoke the experience of loneliness. As you remember these experiences, allow your attention to become focused inward so that you are aware of the sensations of loneliness rather than the apparent causes of it. Take the time to observe how you feel physically when you are lonely. What other feelings surface with the remembrance of loneliness? What thoughts come to you, and what forms does loneliness take in your life?

Describe the experience of loneliness in as much detail as you can.

Physical sensations of loneliness:

Feelings and emotions associated with loneliness:

Thoughts and insights about loneliness:

Images and memories:

Meeting the Teacher of Loneliness

VISUALIZATION 7

Prepare for visualization by following the seven-step visualization process in Preparation for Heartwork (pp. 17–18).

In a state of deep relaxation allow your imagination to envision a safe place where you can meet with loneliness. Allow this teacher to appear in whatever form manifests. You are observing this teacher carefully and taking note of the details of its presence.

What does your loneliness look like?
Do you see any colors or symbols?
If loneliness appeared as a person, what would that person look like?
Male or female?   Age?   Clothing?
Movement, action?

Allow yourself to fully experience this presence. When you sense that you have made a full connection with this teacher, ask your loneliness to speak to you. Speak to your loneliness if you desire to do so.

What is your loneliness communicating to you? What is its message?

When you sense that the dialogue is complete for now, thank this presence for its message and release it. Allow your attention to return to your breathing. Follow the sound and movement of your breath. Become aware of the sounds in your physical environment. Have a sense of fully returning to the room you are in, and when you are ready, open your eyes.

My Experience with the Teacher of Loneliness

Write a detailed description of the appearance of loneliness:

Describe your feelings during this encounter:

Describe the behaviors or actions expressed by loneliness:

My Experience with the Teacher of Loneliness

Record in detail the dialogue that took place between you and loneliness:

Presence

Behind the disguise of loneliness lies the capacity to be present. The absence we feel in the experience of loneliness is a longing we often interpret as the lack of something or someone. We believe that if that absence were filled in a certain way or by a certain form, then the loneliness would ease. In reality there is an absence, but it is we who are missing. Loneliness is an indication that we are refusing to be present with some aspect(s) of our lives. There may be a rejection of a person, a relationship, or a situation that needs our attention. There may be a fear of meeting a certain challenge, telling a certain truth, or a denial of our deeper feelings.

For the purposes of the next exercise, in which we will meet the teacher of presence, choose a situation or relationship from your life in which you find it difficult to be present and fully engaged. Spend the time you need to see this situation or person clearly. What is it that tempts you to withdraw from participating in and giving to this situation?

Practicing Presence

Describe the situation or relationship that you have decided to work with. Include as many aspects of the scenario as you can think of and allow your feelings to surface and to be expressed:

Meeting the Teacher of Presence

Prepare for visualization by following the seven-step visualization process in Preparation for Heartwork (pp. 17–18).

In a state of deep relaxation, with eyes closed, allow your attention to focus again on the safe place where you met with loneliness. Invite the teacher of loneliness to reappear, and when this presence is fully with you, take a few minutes to observe any changes that have taken place in this aspect.

As you are present with your loneliness, allow the situation you are working with to come to your attention, and allow that situation to join you in the safe place where you and your loneliness await. Now you and your teacher are looking together at this situation and contemplating it. You, the teacher, and the situation are together.

As you give this experience your full attention, allow any changes in you, the teacher, or the situation to take place. As these three elements remain together, watch the transformation of your teacher into the teacher of presence and feel the difference in the energy field of that teacher.

What does the teacher of presence look like?
Do you see any colors or symbols?
If presence appeared as a person, what would that person look like?
Male or female?
Age?
Clothing?
Movement, action?

When you feel familiar with the teacher of presence and know that you would recognize the experience of being with this teacher again any time, ask this teacher to communicate with you. What message does the teacher of presence bring? As you listen and understand, you may also ask questions of this teacher. How would this teacher work with the situation that you have brought into its presence with you?

When you sense that the dialogue is complete for now, thank this teacher for its message and release it. Allow your attention to return to your breathing. Follow the sound and movement of your breath, and become aware of the sounds in your environment. Have a sense of fully returning to the room you are in, and when you are ready, open your eyes.

My Experience with the Teacher of Presence

Write a detailed description of the appearance of the teacher of presence:

Describe your feelings during this encounter:

Describe the difference between loneliness and presence:

My Experience with the Teacher of Presence

Record in detail the dialogue between you and the teacher of presence. Describe your understanding of the situation you chose to work with, and write about any new perceptions that occur to you:

Corrupt Power

The issue of power and its misuse in relationships relates to the roles of victim and persecutor or oppressor. Whatever name you would give to the counterpart of the victim aspect, and however you experience yourself in these roles, we come to the heart place to discover the energy and light beneath these destructive images. For the purposes of exploring this chamber, we are going to work with the aspect that engages in the misuse of power through attacking others in any way. Some forms of attack that may come to mind are criticism, sarcasm, ridicule, or a minimizing of another's felt experience. These dynamics in relationships disempower others in an attempt to establish a false sense of power at the expense of Love. In this exercise we are challenging our beliefs about the nature of power, where it is found, and how it is integrated.

Allow yourself to remember a time or situation in your life when you engaged in one or more of these behaviors. If memories of victimization arise, allow them to float by, but maintain your attention on the experience of misusing power through any unkind behavior. As you remember these experiences, allow your attention to become focused on the sensations and feelings that you experience. You are withdrawing your awareness from what you believe were the provocations to these behaviors, and you are remembering the emotions you experienced.

Describe the experience of misusing power in as much detail as you can.

Physical sensations of misusing power:

Feelings and emotions associated with misusing power:

Thoughts and insights about misusing power:

Images and memories:

Meeting the Teacher of Shadow Power

Prepare for visualization by following the seven-step visualization process in Preparation for Heartwork (pp. 17–18).

In a state of deep relaxation allow your imagination to envision a safe place where you can meet with the teacher of shadow power. Allow this teacher to appear in whatever form manifests. You are observing this teacher carefully and taking note of the details of its presence.

> What does shadow power look like?
> Do you see any colors or symbols?
> If this energy appeared as a person, what would that person look like?
> Male or female?   Age?   Clothing?
> Movement, action?

Allow yourself to fully experience this presence. When you sense that you have made a full connection with this teacher, ask this aspect to speak to you. If you choose to do so, you may speak in return.

> What is this desire for power communicating to you? What is its message?

When you sense that the dialogue is complete for now, thank this presence for its message and release it. Allow your attention to return to your breathing. Follow the sound and movement of your breath. Become aware of the sounds of your physical environment. Have a sense of fully returning to the room you are in, and when you are ready, open your eyes.

My Experience with the Teacher of Shadow Power

Write a detailed description of the appearance of shadow power:

Describe your feelings during this encounter with shadow power:

Describe the behaviors or actions expressed by shadow power:

My Experience with the Teacher of Shadow Power

Record in detail the dialogue that took place between you and the teacher of shadow power:

Compassion

Behind the disguise of shadow power lies the essence of true power, compassion. In the search for power in the energy field of another, we are dissociated from the feelings that are the essence of compassion. In reclaiming our deepest feelings and honoring them as guides to our true essence, we are bringing compassion to our own path. Compassion, which is the reverence for the Divinity in all things, acknowledges Love as the only reality as you follow your feelings to the true power within.

Describe the experience of compassion in as much detail as you can.

Physical sensations of compassion:

Feelings and emotions associated with compassion:

Thoughts and insights about compassion:

Images and memories:

Meeting with the Teacher of Compassion

Prepare for visualization by following the seven-step visualization process in Preparation for Heartwork (pp. 17–18).

In a state of deep relaxation, with eyes closed, allow your attention to focus again on the safe place where you met with the teacher of shadow power. Invite this teacher to reappear, and when this presence is fully with you, take a few minutes to observe any changes that have taken place in this aspect.

When you sense that the communication between you is well established, allow your attention to be drawn to the feelings that you are experiencing right now. You are permitting all feelings to arise and move through all levels of your being. No feeling is rejected or judged as you allow them to flow through.

In full awareness of the emotional energy moving through you, you observe the teacher of compassion evolving from shadow power. You are remaining in your felt reality while the teacher of compassion becomes fully present. You are taking note of every detail of the appearance of compassion.

What does compassion look like?

Do you see any colors or symbols?

If compassion came to you as a person, would that person be male or female? Age?

Clothing?

Movement, action?

When you feel completely familiar with the teacher of compassion and know that you would recognize this presence again, ask compassion to speak to you.

If you choose to do so, you may speak to compassion. Experience this dialogue for as long as you wish.

What is compassion communicating to you? What message does this teacher bring?

When you sense that the dialogue is complete for now, thank this teacher for its message of compassion and release it. Allow your attention to return to your breathing. Follow the sound and movement of your breath, and become aware of the sounds in your environment. Have a sense of fully returning to the room you are in, and when you are ready, open your eyes.

My Experience with the Teacher of Compassion

Write a detailed description of the appearance of compassion:

Describe your feelings during this encounter with compassion:

Describe the behaviors or actions expressed by compassion:

My Experience with the Teacher of Compassion

Record in detail the dialogue that took place between you and compassion:

6

Meeting the Teachers of the Front Heart

You will know the joy of seeking, finding, and supporting
the essence of those with whom you share your life.

The Choice for Love
Teachers of the Heart I

As we meet with the teachers of the front heart, we are working with the images of Love that obscure the reality of Love. Caretaking, sympathy, attachment, and helplessness are forms of fear that may be harder to challenge than the forms found in the back heart. They are often more socially acceptable. In questioning these energies in our lives, we are challenging our morality, our imitations of Love, and asking that our sentimentality be replaced with truth. As we meet these disguised teachers, as we courageously unmask our persona, we are redirecting our energy from the external control of behavior and "being good" to the internal issue of intent. We are agreeing to become authentic.

As we become conscious of the true Love behind each image, we are releasing creative energy to deal with the uncomfortable truths and unexpected turns in the path of the heart. We are releasing how we thought Love "should be" in order to discover what it is.

The knowledge of the front heart, when explored and unified with the back heart, becomes the true power of gentleness and harmlessness.

Caretaking

Allow yourself to remember a relationship or situation in which you felt that you had given more than you received, or perhaps felt used and taken advantage of. Perhaps you extended yourself to meet another's needs and felt that you did so at the expense of your own needs. As you remember taking care of this person or situation with a sense of inadequate reciprocation, allow all of your feelings to come to the surface. As you remember your unappreciated sacrifice, allow your attention to move from the situation or person that represents this experience and focus fully on the feelings of sacrifice itself. Take the time to observe how this energy moves through your body. What other feelings surround a sense of sacrifice? What perceptions and beliefs about needs—your needs or the needs of others—come to mind?

Describe the experience of caretaking and sacrifice in as much detail as you can.

Physical sensations of sacrifice:

Feelings and emotions associated with sacrifice:

Thoughts and insights about sacrifice:

Images and memories:

Meeting the Teacher of Caretaking

Prepare for visualization by following the seven-step visualization process in Preparation for Heartwork (pp. 17–18).

In a state of deep relaxation, with eyes closed, allow your inner vision to see a safe place where you can meet with the teacher of caretaking. Allow this presence to appear in whatever form occurs. Take note of the details of its appearance, and bring awareness to your feelings.

What does caretaking look like?
Do you see any colors or symbols?
If caretaking appeared as person, would that person be male or female?
Age?   Clothing?
Movement, action?

Allow yourself to fully experience the energy field of this presence. When you have the feeling that you are familiar enough with caretaking to recognize it any time again, ask this teacher to speak to you. If you wish, you may speak with this teacher. Experience this dialogue for as long as you wish.

What is caretaking communicating to you? What is its message?

When you sense that the dialogue is complete for now, thank this presence for its message and release it. Follow the sound and movement of your breathing, and become aware of the sounds in your physical environment. Have a sense of fully returning to the room you are in, and when you are ready, open your eyes.

My Experience with the Teacher of Caretaking

Write a detailed physical description of the appearance of caretaking:

Describe your feelings during this encounter:

Describe the behaviors or actions of caretaking:

My Experience with the Teacher of Caretaking

Record in detail the dialogue that took place between you and caretaking:

Service

Behind the guise of caretaking and the martyrdom of sacrifice stands the teacher of service. In service the capacity for true giving is free of the perception of need as a basis for relationship. Service rests on the equality of giving and receiving and is free of the contaminant of overresponsibility. In service we demonstrate trust in another's ability to grow and become. The teacher of service guides you to first contacting that which brings you happiness, and then guiding that overflow of joy into actions that serve the best interests of all concerned. The capacity to render genuine service to others and to the planet is a hallmark of the heart in action.

Meeting the Teacher of Service

Prepare for visualization by following the seven-step visualization process in Preparation for Heartwork (pp. 17–18).

In a state of deep relaxation, with eyes closed, allow your attention to focus again on the safe place where you met with caretaking. Invite the teacher of caretaking to reappear, and when this presence is fully with you, take a few minutes to observe any changes that have taken place in this aspect.

When you sense that communication between you is well established, allow yourself to remember something in your life that brings you joy. As you focus on the feeling of joy, allow for the transformation of your teacher as you call forth the energy of service. As the teacher of service is revealed, take note of its appearance and bring awareness to your feelings.

What does service look like?
Do you see any colors or symbols?
If service appeared to you as a person, what would that person look like?
Male or female?
Age?
Clothing?
Movement, action?

When you feel completely familiar with the teacher of service and know that you would recognize this presence again at any time, ask service to speak to you. If you so desire, you may speak to service. Experience this dialogue for as long as you wish.

What does the teacher of service wish to communicate to you? What message does it bring?

When you sense that the dialogue is finished for now, thank this presence for its message and release it. Allow your attention to return to your breathing. Follow the sound and movement of your breath, and become aware of the sounds in your physical environment. Have a sense of fully returning to the room you are in, and when you are ready, open your eyes.

My Experience with the Teacher of Service

Write a detailed description of the appearance of service:

Describe your feelings during this encounter:

Describe the behaviors or actions expressed by service:

My Experience with the Teacher of Service

Record in detail the dialogue that took place between you and service:

Sympathy

Allow yourself to remember a relationship in which you continually "felt sorry for" another person and believed that his or her suffering required special attention from you. Contemplate the manner in which you responded in your efforts to support this person in his or her experience of what seemed to be an unfair and unjust turn of events. How much time and energy did you devote to this person's difficulty, and at what point did you begin to feel drained of energy? What beliefs about suffering are surfacing to consciousness? Allow your attention to move from the situation and person to the felt experience of sympathy. How does this energy move through your body, and what other feelings arise as sympathy moves toward suffering?

Describe the experience of sympathy for suffering in as much detail as you can.

Physical sensations of sympathy:

Feelings and emotions associated with sympathy:

Thoughts and insights about sympathy:

Images and memories:

Meeting the Teacher of Sympathy

VISUALIZATION 13

Prepare for visualization by following the seven-step visualization process in Preparation for Heartwork (pp. 17–18).

In a state of deep relaxation, with eyes closed, allow your inner vision to see a safe place where you can meet with the teacher of sympathy. Allow this presence to appear in whatever form occurs. Take note of the details of this appearance, and bring awareness to your feelings.

What does sympathy look like?
Do you see any colors or symbols?
If sympathy appeared as a person, what would that person look like?
Male or female?   Age?   Clothing?
Movement, action?

Allow yourself to fully experience the energy field of this presence. When you have the sense that you are familiar enough with sympathy to recognize it again at any time, ask this teacher to speak to you, and if you desire, you may speak to it. Experience this dialogue for as long as you wish.

What is sympathy communicating to you? What is its message?

When you sense that the dialogue is complete for now, thank this presence for its message and release it. Follow the sound and movement of your breathing, and become aware of the sounds in your physical environment. Have a sense of fully returning to the room you are in, and when you are ready, open your eyes.

My Experience with the Teacher of Sympathy

Write a detailed description of the appearance of sympathy:

Describe your feelings during this encounter:

Describe the behaviors or actions of sympathy:

My Experience with the Teacher of Sympathy

Record in detail the dialogue that took place between you and sympathy:

Empathy

Behind the guise of sympathy and the belief in suffering stands the teacher of empathy. Rather than focusing on misery and impotence, empathy searches for and finds the genuine strengths, talents, and gifts of another. Rather than viewing life challenges as tragic, empathy is aware of the light of the soul that illuminates the lessons we came to learn. The teacher of empathy will remind you that while you may honor the genuine struggle of the human path, deep within we all have the creative energy and strength of spirit necessary to deal constructively with apparent setbacks. Empathy affirms this power and supports the true essence of another.

Meeting the Teacher of Empathy

VISUALIZATION 14

Prepare for visualization by following the seven-step visualization process in Preparation for Heartwork (pp. 17–18).

In a state of deep relaxation, with your eyes closed, allow your attention to focus again on the safe place where you met with sympathy. Invite the teacher of sympathy to reappear, and when this presence is fully with you, take a few minutes to observe any changes that have taken place in this aspect.

When you sense that communication between you is well established, allow yourself to envision a person for whom you have shown sympathy in the past. See that person very clearly. Now you and sympathy are looking together at that person. As you look together, focus your attention on this person's strengths, gifts, and talents. Allow these aspects of the person to become very clear in your mind. As you do so, watch for the transformation of sympathy into the teacher of empathy. As the teacher of empathy is revealed, bring your attention to the appearance of empathy.

What does empathy look like?
Do you see any colors or symbols?
If empathy appeared to you as a person, what would that person look like?
Male or female?
Age?
Clothing?
Movement, action?

When you feel completely comfortable with the teacher of empathy and know that you would recognize this presence again at any time, ask empathy to speak to you. If you wish, you may speak to empathy. Experience this dialogue for as long as you wish.

What does the teacher of empathy communicate to you? What message does it bring?

When you sense that the dialogue is finished for now, thank this presence for its message and release it. Allow your attention to return to your breathing. Follow the sound and movement of your breath, and become aware of the sounds in your physical environment. Have a sense of fully returning to the room you are in, and when you are ready, open your eyes.

My Experience with the Teacher of Empathy

Write a detailed description of the appearance of empathy:

Describe your feelings during this encounter:

Describe the behaviors or actions expressed by empathy:

My Experience with the Teacher of Empathy

Record in detail the dialogue that took place between you and empathy:

Attachment

Allow yourself to remember a relationship or situation in which you often feared that you would lose what you had gained. Contemplate the experience of needing that person or that situation in order to feel safe and secure. Allow yourself to be conscious of whatever it is you believe you cannot live without. See the many forms that your need is attached to. As you think of these objects of attachment, allow all of your feelings to come to the surface. As you call to mind what you believe are necessities, allow your attention to move from these images to the felt experience of attachment. Take the time to observe how this energy moves through your body. What other feelings surround the sensations of attachment? As you deeply experience your feelings, what other images appear?

Describe the experience of attachment in as much detail as you can.

Physical sensations of attachment:

Feelings and emotions associated with attachment:

Thoughts and insights about attachment:

Images and memories:

Meeting the Teacher of Attachment

Prepare for visualization by following the seven-step visualization process in Preparation for Heartwork (pp. 17–18).

In a state of deep relaxation, with eyes closed, allow your inner vision to see a safe place where you can meet with the teacher of attachment. Allow this presence to appear in whatever form occurs. Take note of the details of its appearance, and bring awareness to your feelings.

What does attachment look like?
Do you see any colors or symbols?
If attachment appeared to you as a person, what would that person look like?
Male or female?   Age?   Clothing?
Movement, action?

Allow yourself to fully experience the energy field of this presence. When you have the sense that you are familiar enough with this presence to recognize it again at any time, ask this teacher to speak to you, and if you desire, speak to attachment. Experience this dialogue for as long as you wish.

What is attachment communicating to you? What is its message?

When you sense that the dialogue is complete for now, thank this presence for its message and release it. Follow the sound and movement of your breathing, and become aware of the sounds in your physical environment. Have a sense of fully returning to the room you are in, and when you are ready, open your eyes.

My Experience with the Teacher of Attachment

Write a detailed description of the appearance of attachment:

Describe your feelings during this encounter:

Describe the behaviors or actions of attachment:

My Experience with the Teacher of Attachment

Record in detail the dialogue that took place between you and attachment:

Freedom

Behind the guise of attachment and fear of loss stands the teacher of freedom. This teacher invites us to move beyond the limits we have established on what we will receive from the limitless bounty of the Universe. Rather than focusing on the prevention of loss by controlling that which we believe we need, the teacher of freedom expands into unknown possibilities of potential. In freedom our creative energy is released from keeping what little we have to letting go into greater abundance at all levels. In freedom of will is the power of choice then raised to consciousness. Attachment to an external source becomes redirected to accessing the internal Source, which is ours forever and which we cannot lose.

Meeting the Teacher of Freedom

VISUALIZATION 16

Prepare for visualization by following the seven-step visualization process in Preparation for Heartwork (pp. 17–18).

In a state of deep relaxation, with your eyes closed, allow your attention to focus again on the safe place where you met with attachment. Invite the teacher of attachment to reappear, and when this presence is fully with you, take a few minutes to observe any changes that have taken place in this aspect.

When you sense that communication between you is well established, allow yourself to look at one aspect of your life that you are afraid may change. See this object of your attachment very clearly. Now you and the teacher of attachment are looking at this aspect together. As you continue to look, concentrate on opening your hands. As your hands open and relax, watch for the revealing of the teacher of freedom. As your hands remain free and loose, you are bringing your attention to the appearance of freedom.

What does freedom look like?

Do you see any colors or symbols?

If freedom came to you as a person, what would that person look like?

Male or female?

Age?

Clothing?

Movement, action?

When you feel completely comfortable with the teacher of freedom and know that you would recognize this presence again at any time, ask freedom to speak to you. If you wish, you may speak to freedom. Experience this dialogue for as long as you want.

What does the teacher of freedom communicate to you? What message does it bring?

When you sense that the dialogue is complete for now, thank this presence for its message and release it. Allow your attention to return to your breathing. Follow the sound and movement of your breath, and become aware of the sounds in your physical environment. Have a sense of fully returning to the room you are in, and when you are ready, open your eyes.

My Experience with the Teacher of Freedom

Write a detailed description of the appearance of freedom:

Describe your feelings during this encounter:

Describe the behaviors or actions expressed by freedom:

My Experience with the Teacher of Freedom

Record in detail the dialogue that took place between you and freedom:

Helplessness

Allow yourself to remember a situation or relationship in which you frequently felt helpless, unable to cope, and unable to deal adequately with the challenges presented. Allow yourself to remember, without judgment, any denial or avoidance of the situation. Did you try to obscure the difficulty with false optimism? Did you feel that you had no choice? Did you believe that you were the innocent and injured party? Were you trying to resolve the situation by "being nice" or by staying out of the way? Did it evoke the need for hiding any talents or gifts you might have brought to the situation? Were you unable to act from a sense of self-worth? Does it remind you of the powerlessness of childhood? Allow your attention to move from the situation or relationship and bring your awareness to the feeling of helplessness. How does this energy move through your body? What other feelings accompany a sense of powerlessness, lack of choice, and lack of energy?

Describe the experience of helplessness in as much detail as you can.

Physical sensations of helplessness:

Feelings and emotions associated with helplessness:

Thoughts and insights about helplessness:

Images and memories:

Meeting the Teacher of Helplessness

Prepare for visualization by following the seven-step visualization process in Preparation for Heartwork (pp. 17–18).

In a state of deep relaxation, with eyes closed, allow your inner vision to see a safe place where you can meet with the teacher of helplessness. Allow this presence to appear in whatever form occurs. Take note of the details of this appearance, and bring awareness to your feelings.

What does helplessness look like?

Do you see any colors or symbols?

If helplessness appeared as a person, what would that person look like?

Male or female?   Age?   Clothing?

Movement, action?

Allow yourself to fully experience the energy field of this presence. When you have the sense that you are familiar enough with helplessness to recognize it again at any time, ask this teacher to speak to you. Speak to helplessness if you so desire. Experience this dialogue for as long as you wish.

What is helplessness communicating to you? What is its message?

When you sense that the dialogue is complete for now, thank this presence for its message and release it. Return your attention to your breathing, and follow its sound and movement. Become aware of the sounds in your physical environment. Have a sense of fully returning to the room you are in, and when you are ready, open your eyes.

My Experience with the Teacher of Helplessness

Write a detailed description of the appearance of helplessness:

Describe your feelings during this encounter:

Describe the behaviors or actions of helplessness:

My Experience with the Teacher of Helplessness

Record in detail the dialogue that took place between you and helplessness:

Surrender

Behind the guise of helplessness and feelings of inadequacy stands the teacher of surrender. This teacher comes with the lessons of true power. Unlike helplessness, which gives in and gives up, surrender is an agreement to equal partnership. The false humility and self-devaluation of helplessness is released as we accept personal responsibility for our gifts, our talents, and our Divine Nature. Rather than giving our power away to people, circumstances, and events, we become conscious of what is truly ours to give, and we consult our hearts as to where to give it. If we believe we are not worthy, we believe we have nothing to offer. If we surrender to our own light and the Light of the Universe, we know that we have everything to give. Surrender is empowering because it is an agreement to move with the energy of Divine Law.

Meeting the Teacher of Surrender

Prepare for visualization by following the seven-step visualization process in Preparation for Heartwork (pp. 17–18).

In a state of deep relaxation, with your eyes closed, allow your attention to focus again on the safe place where you met with helplessness. Invite the teacher of helplessness to reappear, and when this presence is fully with you, take a few minutes to observe any changes that have taken place in this aspect.

When you sense that the communication between you is well established, allow yourself to see again the relationship or situation in which you felt unable to cope. Now you and helplessness are looking at this together. As the two of you contemplate this, allow yourself to remember clearly a talent or gift that you have. It could be very simple, such as the ability to cook a wonderful meal or to make someone laugh. Feel the joy of being in that talent, and as you do so, watch for the transformation of your teacher. As the teacher of surrender is revealed, bring your attention to the appearance of surrender.

What does surrender look like?

Do you see any colors or symbols?

If surrender appeared to you as a person, what would that person look like?

Male or female?

Age?

Clothing?

Movement, action?

When you feel completely comfortable with the teacher of surrender and know that you would recognize this presence again at any time, ask surrender to speak to you. If you so desire, speak to surrender. Experience this dialogue for as long as you wish.

What does the teacher of surrender communicate to you? What is its message?

When you sense that the dialogue is finished for now, thank this presence for its message and release it. Allow your attention to return to your breathing, and follow the sound and movement of your breath. Become aware of the sounds in your physical environment. Have a sense of fully returning to the room you are in, and when you are ready, open your eyes.

My Experience with the Teacher of Surrender

Write a detailed description of the appearance of surrender:

Describe your feelings during this encounter:

Describe the behaviors or actions expressed by surrender:

My Experience with the Teacher of Surrender

Record in detail the dialogue that took place between you and surrender:

Now that you have met with the teachers of the front heart and back heart, you are aware of the energies of those presences. You will have many opportunities in your daily life to recognize these teachers and the lessons they assist you to learn.

It is your complete acceptance of your human path, with all of its universal temptations and choices, that acquaints you with the teachers of the heart, that allows them to come forth from their disguises to teach you and assist you, that transforms the blocks to Love into the open doorways to truth.

The Choice for Love
Teachers of the Heart II

7

Wholeheartedness

The union of the front and back heart, through the way of forgiveness,
brings the heart into its full capacity to love and to engage the power
of Love. . . . From this internal unity, our unity with all stands
apparent and real. From this unity, the creations of Love are born.

The Choice for Love
Wholeheartedness

As we continue to learn from the teachers of the back heart and front heart, we become aware of the need to heal the breach between them. The gap between the two halves of the sanctuary requires a bridge so that communication between the front and back heart can be established. This bridge is built by your practices of forgiveness. These practices are *nonjudgment* and *nonviolence.* In fully engaging in your challenges and relationships, you will have many opportunities to apply these practices until they evolve from a conscious discipline to a way of life. These exercises are tools that can be applied repeatedly to any person, relationship, or situation. Your life, which is your healing, provides many opportunities to practice.

Nonjudgment

The relinquishment of judgment is the acknowledgement that we cannot know all there is to know about any person, circumstance, or situation. The experience of not-knowing is our first engagement with truth. Without our prejudices, our morality, our need for information, or the evaluations of "right" and "wrong," the resulting open-mindedness leaves room for revelation. In choosing non-judgment, we become aware of our judgments. They are raised to consciousness so that we may choose again, so that we may release them.

For the following exercises, choose a person, a relationship, or a situation that you have rejected either partially or totally. Allow yourself to contemplate all aspects of this situation, including all of your feelings, and explore these aspects as fully as you can. As previously, you will be using the guidelines provided on each page, but allow yourself to record anything else that comes to consciousness.

What I know about this person, relationship, or situation: →

What I appreciate about this person, relationship, or situation (find at least three aspects of appreciation): →

← *What I don't know about this person, relationship, or situation:*

← *What I criticize or judge about this person, relationship, or situation:*

How I feel when I am in appreciation:

How am I different from the other(s) in this situation?

← *How I feel when I am in judgment:*

← *How am I the same as the other(s) in this situation?*

*As you experience both judgment and nonjudgment in this exercise, →
what new insights or perceptions are present?*

*If you remained in nonjudgment, how might this person, relationship, or →
situation change?*

← *What judgments about yourself would you like to release?*

← *If you released judgments about yourself, how might your life change?*

Nonviolence

Nonviolence is a practice of forgiveness that challenges your beliefs in suffering and justified attack. Nonviolence is a refusal to give faith to the illusions of harm and defense.

If we believe we are harmed, we misperceive ourselves as victims. If we then offer harm to "protect" ourselves, we believe that violence is an answer.

The practices of nonviolence and nonjudgment go hand in hand. If without judgment we see no victims, no persecutors, then we are free from these oppressive roles, these false identities. We open the prison door, and we release ourselves from the powerlessness of anger in order to discover who we are behind these illusions. With the practice of nonviolence we connect with the Spiritual Law of harmlessness. Harmlessness is true power because in the face of fear, it stands in Love. In Love you remember who you are.

For the purposes of the following exercises, choose a person, relationship, or situation in which you perceived yourself as either harmed, or having done harm, or both. Allow yourself to remember clearly all that you perceived and all that you felt and continue to feel. As you are prompted in your journaling by the guidelines on each page, allow yourself to record anything else that comes to consciousness.

How I believe I was harmed in this relationship or situation: →

How did this relationship or situation shape my view of myself? →

← *How I believe that I did harm in this relationship or situation:*

← *How did I view the other person(s) in this relationship or situation?*

If I had written the script for this relationship or situation as an onstage →
drama, what role did I play?

When did I play this role before, and what are my feelings in this →
identity?

| *Heartwork*

← *If I had written the script for this relationship or situation as an onstage drama, what role(s) did I give the other(s)?*

← *When did the other(s) play this role before, and what are my feelings about them?*

If I were to rewrite this play, what role could I play that would bring →
me joy?

If harm were impossible, what message would this play convey? →

←   *If I were to rewrite this play, what role could I give the other(s) that would bring me joy?*

←   *If harm were impossible, what message would I receive?*

If it were impossible that I could ever harm another, who would I be?

If it were impossible that another could ever harm me, who would the other be?

If I could create the life I wanted, what would that life look like?

PART III

HEART IN RELATIONSHIP

When you are in union and you are creating,
you too are sharing your essence.
This is the human expression of Love.

The Choice for Love
The Course of Love

8

The Course of Love

As you integrate the aspects of your human self and experience through consciousness and compassion, the resulting Third Energy produces the sacred space where you personally meet and commune with Spirit. It is here where you receive truthful guidance for your life path, which, if followed, leads you to the fulfillment of your highest potential for inventiveness and service.

The Choice for Love
The Course of Love

Just as the union of male and female gives birth to a third person, a child, so too union of any two energies, whatever form they take, produces a Third Energy. As the child is unique, conscious, and creative, so too the Third Energy is alive with consciousness and creativity. Following this consciousness is the path of the heart. This consciousness, which resides in the dimension of soul, delivers its messages from the Divine to the heart.

Your work in the front heat, back heart, and your practices of forgiveness clear your intuitive channels. The heart that has been healed and unified holds the knowledge of how to create from Love. This wholeheartedness is the key to the fulfillment of your heart's desire and is the seat of courage necessary to move into the unknown, to follow your highest path. The relinquishment of control for the walk of faith is guided by the Third Energy.

The following exercises will help you to explore where you may experience blocks to either receiving intuitive messages through the heart or following the guidance once received. As these blocks are cleared, the Third Energy is less of a mystery and more of a felt and knowable source of truth and direction.

Writing at least ten thoughts very quickly and without any editing, finish the following sentence.

If I had no fear I would:

Allow yourself to contemplate a relationship or situation that is troubling you at this time. Allow yourself to be conscious of all the aspects involved and all the feelings that you experience when considering this challenge. As previously, you will be using the guidelines provided on each page, but allow yourself to record any other insights that surface.

Ways that I have tried to resolve the issues involved in this situation or relationship: →

My plans for today: →

← *Concerning this relationship or situation, if I had no fear, I would:*

← *What I really want to do today:*

Experiences I have had while following my plans to the letter: →

How I feel when following my plans: →

← *Experiences I have had that were spontaneous and unplanned:*

← *How I feel when being spontaneous:*

Situations in which I play it safe: →

My expectations and goals for my life: →

← *Situations in which I am willing to take risks:*

← *My wildest dreams for my life:*

Ways to Experiment with the Third Energy

Ask a friend with whom you are very comfortable to participate in these experiments with you.

1. You are doing a drawing together. You have paper and pastels or whatever medium you choose to draw with. You work without any verbal communication with one another. One draws briefly, sits back, and the other then draws. Each follows an intuitive sense of when to stop and allow the other to take a turn. When you both sense that the project is finished, talk together about the drawing and any insights or feelings you experienced.

2. You and your friend spend a day together that is completely unplanned. The only goal is joy. You agree to spontaneously follow a moment-by-moment unfolding, deciding as you go along what to do and where to go. You create only what you completely agree upon, and if differences arise, you patiently listen to one another until you find something that both genuinely want to do. After the experiment is completed, share with one another any insights and feelings that surfaced for both of you.

3. You and your friend decide to do something that you have never done but have always wanted to do. Holding a joint vision, together you create the ways and means to do it. Choose something simple to begin with. Allow the vision to develop and become, and be flexible as to the means for accomplishment. Stay alert and aware to the unexpected assistance you receive.

9

The Romantic Relationship—Mirror of the Path

*Everyone in your life, without exception, is a companion on the path
to Love and is a partner in your lessons and your potential for creation.
In every relationship lies the possibility of the healing of the heart,
the Call to Love, and the form of extension that is
the manifestation of the Divine on Earth.*

The Choice for Love
Cycle of Healing

In this section of *Heartwork*, you will be exploring the deeper meaning of relationship as the healing arena of the heart. As a relationship evolves and grows, it moves through four stages, which mirror the stages of the healing process. These stages are not fixed and linear, but rather are cycled through again and again in ever-deepening explorations of healing and self-knowledge. These stages are

(1) The heart opens;
(2) Working with the blocks to Love;
(3) Communication from the heart;
(4) Extension.

One of the most common forms of moving through—or blocking—these four stages, and one that most of us share, is the romantic relationship. The romantic relationship mirrors the healing path, but so does every other relationship. The relationships between and among parent-child, student-teacher, friends, siblings, and coworkers are all forms of explorations of the deeper meaning of Love. We pay attention to the romantic relationship because of its compelling passion and its presence in the forefront of our awareness.

For the purposes of raising to consciousness your experience of these stages, choose one relationship in which you are or were passionately involved. You may have judged this relationship as either a success or failure, but these judgments are meaningless. There is only learning. As you come to realize where you habitually block the course of Love, resist the temptation to condemn yourself. Remember that as the blocks are raised to awareness, you are touching your power to remove those blocks.

As you work with these exercises, following the guidelines on each page, allow yourself to record any other insights that also arise.

Stage 1: The Heart Opens

As you remember the beginning stages of the relationship you have chosen to work with, you are recalling the sense of ecstasy and union you experienced as your heart opened in love for another.

Describe in detail all the feelings you experienced during this heart opening (e.g., safety, security, joy, trust, freedom, fearlessness, confidence, etc.):

What were my perceptions of myself during this period of opening? →

How did I feel about our differences? →

← What were my perceptions of the other during this period of opening?

← How did I feel about our similarities?

What did I receive in this opening? →

What visions did I have for my life at this time? →

←   *What did I give in this opening?*

←   *What inner strengths, talents, and gifts did I discover at this time?*

Stage 2: Working with the Blocks to Love

In stage 2 the heart, which has been opened, seizes the opportunity to heal by revealing its hidden recesses of pain and fear. The wisdom of the heart is working to heal the past in the present moment by raising to consciousness all the barriers we place on the path to Love. Here we work with our projections and our tendency to blame either ourselves or the other.

Describe the period during which you were "disillusioned" in this relationship and write all of your feelings about this experience:

For what did I blame myself in this relationship? →

How did I defend myself or take distance in this relationship? →

←　*For what did I blame the other?*

←　*How did the other defend him/herself or take distance in this relationship?*

What grief issues surfaced during this period? →

What did I do to preserve the outer form of this relationship? →

| *Heartwork*

← *How did I handle the grief that I felt?*

← *What did I do to preserve the essence of love and truth in this relationship?*

What were my perceptions of myself during this period?

What were my perceptions of the other during this period?

Stage 3: Communication from the Heart

In stage 3 we are invited to enter into deeper levels of communication than we are normally accustomed to. The challenge at this stage is to come out of hiding and to release our attachment to certain roles and behaviors. We release the need to conduct the relationship on "automatic pilot," and bring increased awareness and authentic emotional honesty to our partner. Communication from the heart, based on nonjudgment and nonviolence, goes far beyond literal honesty into the heart of the unknown in our self and the other.

Describe the patterns of communication in the relationship:

What I felt safe to communicate about in this relationship: →

What was the purpose I set for communicating with my partner? →

← *What I felt unsafe to communicate about:*

← *How was that purpose fulfilled in our communication?*

What did I appreciate about communicating with my partner? →

What intention do I choose to set for communicating with my partner? →

← *What did I wish had been different in our communications?*

← *If my intention had been unity, how would that change the way I communicated?*

What areas of feeling did I open to my partner?

What new areas of feeling would I like to open to my partner?

Stage 4: Extension

Extension refers to the creative endeavors and accomplishments that result from the union of two or more people. This extension beyond the boundaries of the two in relationship is a sharing of the creative energy of that union with others. It is a positive contribution to the relationship itself and to the planet as a whole.

List all the things you created with your partner (everything from the simplest, such as cooking a meal together, to the larger projects you created together):

What is easy for my partner and me to create together? →

What passions do we share and work together on? →

← *What is difficult for my partner and me to create together?*

← *What individual passions do we express and cultivate?*

What have I accomplished with my partner that I could never have done alone? →

How has past tradition served our creative process? →

← *What new creations would I like to explore with my partner?*

← *How might breaking with tradition serve our creative process?*

PART IV

THE CHOICE FOR LOVE

*You are awakening, and you can no longer claim to be
unaware of your true power to create your own life. . . .
You see the possibilities for creating along the lines of Love
and what it will mean in terms of changing your life.*

The Choice for Love
Rest for the Heart

IO

Rest for the Heart

Rest at all levels—physical, emotional, mental
and spiritual—is a vital part of any journey.
It is a time of integration, restoration, contemplation.

The Choice for Love
Rest for the Heart

In this section of *Heartwork,* you will be exploring the ways in which you can find rest from the struggle on the path from fear to Love. These resting places, these respites from a challenging journey, are *gratitude, the present moment,* and *silence.* Compassion for ourselves allows us to respect, without judgment, the limits of being human. To rest is to remember that our life is in much Higher Hands than our own, and that time for contemplation of new knowledge and experience is also time for growth. In the resting places of the heart, we relinquish our performance ethic and our need to control the outcome of any situation. As you enter these resting places more and more frequently, you hone your ability to hear the wisdom and guidance of your heart. In these sanctuaries, as you integrate the lessons of the heart, the resulting unity creates the sacred space for the Third Energy. It is here that you commune directly with Spirit and learn the path of your highest potential.

The following exercises are given to you to explore these resting places, which may be accessed at any time and under any circumstances. As with all the previous exercises, you will be working with specific situations. With practice, these exercises become tools for use in all circumstances.

Gratitude

The practice of gratitude is a discipline that precedes the feeling of gratitude. The feeling of gratitude is one of the most blissful in our human experience, but very often it is confined and limited to people, outcomes, and circumstances we think we like. The heart encompassment of gratitude evolves from our distinctions between negative and positive to include every experience in our acceptance and appreciation. It is a decision and an agreement that there is nothing in our life that does not serve Love's purpose.

Make a list of everything in your life that brings you joy:

Make a list of everything in your life that you wish would change: →

Describe the challenges that you personally experience in this relationship or situation: →

← *Choose a relationship or situation from your second list to work with.*
Describe this relationship or situation, and all of your feelings about it:

← *How are these challenges perfect for you right now?*

What am I learning about myself in this relationship or situation?   →

What chamber(s) and teacher(s) of my heart are being activated by   →
this relationship or situation?

← *What strengths and talents are being called upon and developed in this relationship or situation?*

← *How is this relationship or situation perfect right now for my growth into greater Love?*

The Present Moment

Coming into the present moment is a way to be with your heart, because the heart, like the soul, rests in the present moment. This is the practice of union with your own feelings and inner experience as well as with your external world. It is this union that soothes the heart.

While you are journaling in these exercises, bring your awareness to your breathing. Consciously direct the breath to well below the upper chest into the solar plexus and lower belly. Notice how the heartbeat slows down and how your body relaxes in this breath. If you notice that the breath is speeding up and becoming shallow, gently deepen the breath and continue the exercise.

Describe in detail all of the elements of your physical environment that →
are within your line of vision at the present moment:

Describe all of the thoughts that are crossing your mind at the present →
moment:

← *Describe all of the feelings that arise as you contemplate your physical environment:*

← *Describe all of the feelings that accompany your thoughts at the present moment:*

Describe the images and pictures that are appearing to your inner eye at the present moment:

Heartwork

Describe all of the feelings that accompany those images and pictures at the present moment:

Silence

The practice of silence enables the heart to rest and will also raise to consciousness what disturbs the heart. The heart's peace can be disrupted by noise at all levels—physical, mental, emotional, and spiritual. The temptation to avoid silence at any or all of these levels is a fear of emptiness, and indicates a belief in and dependence upon outside sources to nourish or guide us. The practice of silence and accompanying solitude is crucial for the resting and strengthening of the heart and the deeper walk with Spirit.

In each of the following exercises, you will be asked to prepare for your journaling by setting aside one day to practice silence at these levels. After each day, at each level, write about your experiences while they are still fresh in your mind.

Physical Silence

Set aside one day in which you arrange to eliminate as much physical noise as possible from your environment, including television, radio, telephone, any electrical equipment, conversation, traffic, or any other form of external noise that you can think of.

What I found difficult about having a day of physical silence:

What I enjoyed about having a day of physical silence:

Mental Silence

Set aside another day that includes physical silence, and add to that an exploration of mental silence. Along with the elimination of television and radio, you eliminate all reading materials and anything that is intellectually stimulating.

What I learned about myself while being alone with my thoughts:

Which thoughts brought me joy and peace?

Emotional Silence

Set aside another day of physical and mental silence in which you eliminate any coping mechanisms you use to repress your feelings, such as overeating or overactivity, etc.

What was challenging for me in being in silent company with my feelings?

What was helpful for me in being in silent company with my feelings?

Spiritual Silence

Set aside another day of physical, mental, and emotional silence in which your attention is focused on your breath and the movement of your body. A walk in nature is a very helpful tool for this exercise, in which the mind is focused on breath and movement, enabling you to hear messages from your heart.

How did my heart communicate with me during my day of silence (images, deep thoughts, feelings, symbols, inner voice)?

What guidance did I receive for my life right now?

II

Deepening Compassion

*Compassion is a form of sharing. What you share
is the only thing you can share—and that is your essence,
your true Self, your Divine Nature.*

The Choice for Love
Heart Beat—Extending the Rhythms of Love

Compassion is much more than a blissful feeling or the performance of good works. It is the quintessential expression of integrity, because it is based on Self-revelation. It is the sharing of and reverence for our deepest struggles and our Highest Nature. There are two stages to the development of compassion. The first is communication from the heart, in which we allow the uncovering of our shadow in the safety of a committed relationship. The second stage is a further coming out of hiding as we acknowledge our gifts and talents and use them in service to our self and others.

Communication from the Heart

What am I open about in the most intimate relationship of my life? →

What would be threatened if I shared my secret(s) with another? →

← *What secrets do I still keep in the most intimate relationship of my life?*

← *What would be free if I shared my secret(s) with another?*

Gifts and Talents

What are my gifts and talents? →

If I were to express these gifts and talents fully, what would change in my life? →

← *How much and how often do I allow these gifts and talents to be expressed?*

← *How do I feel about these possible changes?*

What gifts and talents bring me the greatest joy?

How could my gifts and talents serve those who are in my life?

Epilogue

The Highest Law

It is this path that we take together, a path that transcends
apparent differences of culture, race, religion, and experience.
In the heart we share a sanctuary where all are one in purpose
and understanding, where our unity with one another and
the Divine shape and empower our intent for peace
and our prayer for Love.

The Choice for Love
The Highest Law

Blessings on all of you courageous ones who have completed this workbook and who have directed your free will towards compassion, to raise to consciousness the choice between fear and Love. This choice will be with you till the end of your journey as you evolve into deeper and deeper levels of understanding and Self-knowledge.

May you continue to give yourselves deepest compassion as you offer an imperfect life to perfect healing. May your heart grow strong in unity as you are guided into the joyous service on this planet that will be your unique contribution to all of us.

Love, Maggie

The final word is yours . . .

My Prayer for the Path of My Heart:

About Maggie Victor

After practicing her profession of nursing in the fields of psychiatry and pediatrics, Maggie Victor established a private practice in counseling, mandala work, and aromatherapy. In addition to assisting in the healing process of individuals, she has led many workshops and women's groups and has developed both a communications program and a unique form of group mandala work designed to open deeper levels of communication through creativity.

Maggie's original methods of working with people led to corporate consulting for companies who were searching for ways to develop the potential of individual employees, as well as that of the corporation. She has also taught courses in yoga and meditation and designed well-attended weekend workshops based on the teachings of "A Course in Miracles." Maggie wrote a regular feature for *Elle Quebec* called "Vie Intérieure" ("The Inner Life"), which received strong reader response. She lives in Beaconsfield, Quebec.